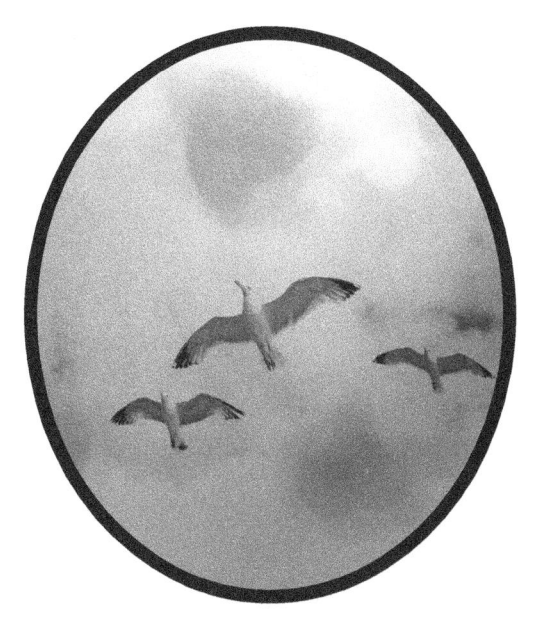

FLEDGES AND
PHRASELINGS

JASON HOLT

ANAPHORA LITERARY PRESS

QUANAH, TEXAS

ANAPHORA LITERARY PRESS
1108 W 3rd Street
Quanah, TX 79252
https://anaphoraliterary.com

Book design by Anna Faktorovich, Ph.D.

Published in 2019 by Anaphora Literary Press

Fledges and Phraselings
Jason Holt—1st edition.

Library of Congress Control Number: 2019906508

Library Cataloging Information
Holt, Jason, 1971-, author.
    Fledges and phraselings / Jason Holt
    76 p. ; 9 in.
    ISBN 978-1-68114-502-0 (softcover : alk. paper)
    ISBN 978-1-68114-503-7 (hardcover : alk. paper)
    ISBN 978-1-68114-504-4 (e-book)
1. Poetry—Canadian. 2. Poetry—Subjects & Themes—Places.
3. Philosophy—Ethics & Moral Philosophy.
PN6099-6110: Collections of general literature: Poetry
191: Philosophy of United States and Canada

CONTENTS

THIS POEM IS A CAT

this poem
is a cat
it sleeps
in the pike position
it curls
around its concern
it yawns
in the face
of any criticism
or praise
but isn't above
a closedeye purr
when stroked

A Distinctly Cleared Throat

it sounds
a little too esque
to be
stepping out
from the shadow
of its own cliché
difficult
as a squint
beyond
the deep voice
as yet unheard
the film cutting
silent black
at a distinctly
cleared throat

Such a Yawned Emotion

could such a yawned emotion
as missing my wife
even at martini night
the light an icy shadow
on this page
through the cocktail glass
even as this man
pushes fifty
less but still given
to such accessful youth
as absence sharpens against
the night itself
alone with the family cat
in a house the mortgage fully paid
even at the distance
of visiting beyond
another province sisters
even with a full year
sabbatical's approach
the stack of term papers
to mark dwindling apace
viscous as a canadian spring
even as I sit back
against the pull of slouch
smiled on by my diminishing glass
in front of what's behind
a face I didn't shave today

NOT EVEN THE CHRISTMASLIGHTS

at times like this
not even
the christmaslights
can help

THE POEM I DIDN'T WRITE

dovetailed
or raventailed
that
was the poem
I didn't write
but should have
this
the comment
I shouldn't make
but do

LaGuardia Airport,
Terminal B, Almost 3 a.m.

laguardia airport
terminal b
almost three a m
the zombified
have slept
at the free chairless
food court
the small one
that's open
for how many
whose eternities
the free shuttles
still running though
as if at a or c or d
it somehow promised more
but having run
that gamut I sit
on this air canada
luggage belt
as if a business class
desperation
could justify
this hours long
nowhere else
with that
my current weight

HER LET'S SAY PASSION

do the wrinkles
in this notebook
in this mirrored face
in her
let's say passion
suggest
I need a new one
I can't recall
what moisture
what weather or time
produced them

PRETENSE OF A GESTURE

this is a poem
whose only pretense
of a gesture
at virtue
is the freedom
its banner waves
in pride
of lacking any
much less significant
form

THE WHOLE POINT OF THE BACKPACK

the whole point
of the backpack
is not to overfill it
or to approach
that emptiness
that makes
only the apparent
burden light
selection is the key
the touch
that lights significance
or foreknowledge how
unfolds contingency

THIS QUESTIONMARK ROAD

savage noble
more like it
what soft
connective tissue
this
what last ditches
bordering
this questionmark
road

An Argument of Philosophers

a murder
of crows
an argument
of philosophers

A Poem in Self-Referential Vein

a poem in self-referential vein
unfolding as a flower might its face
arterial its lifeblood to regain
in pumping forth sonnetic and apace
the formlessness of most enchanted life
its rhythm half itself half metered verse
in losing or in winning from the strife
a goodly better best that worsens worse
another rhythm dance and music both
embodied one the other all abstract
between the two an earnest-taken oath
envisioning a balance then enact
however brief coherent and intense
resolving all in giving life its sense

A Theory of Hamlet

a theory of hamlet
the reason he can't act
isn't indecision
but that the fool
must be played
and he
since yorick is dead
must play
the fool himself
and by definition
the fool can't act
only comment
on the action
and make in such jesting
the action of life itself
almost bearable

THIS FOOTNOTE EXISTENCE

is it back then
to this
this footnote
existence

THE BEAUTY THAT ELUDES

the beauty
that eludes
the perfect poem
at the very peak
of the greatest bard
a mountain
enshadowing
this beach
whose erosion
nears complete

A Rose as Any Other Symbol

a rose
as any
other
symbol
would not
smell
as sweet

Love as a Paradox

love
is a paradox
of mutual
humility
I thought
before
I ever felt

THIN WITTICISMS

do these little
half committed to
thin witticisms
make up
for any loss
any failure
a handful
of scattered earth
in an open grave

If I Knew Tomorrow

if I knew
tomorrow
what I know
today
I wouldn't try
to write
this book

THE DIVINE ELSEWHERE

how many times
a lifetime
the whole
what it's worth
the part
never played
or played too well
or just right
but all alone
with all eyes
even the divine
elsewhere

PRO RE E GRESS

shoulda
woulda
coulda
buddha

A Phraseling or Two

that this
my latest effort
to conceive
a phraseling
or two
absent
genuine offspring
could
for something
or something else
almost
make up

ANY FLEDGE MANY

but then
from all
these phraselings
how if any
fledges many
flying flown
beyond their own
not
but something
quite

My Chest Is Just a Fist

my chest
is just
a fist at this
point
of almost
no return
wagered
once more
for keeps
and not
a keepsake's
worth

PASCAL'S OR SOME COMPULSIVE'S

but you ask
what kind of wager
not pascal's
or some compulsive's
rather
in this shivering
a glimpse
of sunlight trace
but
from where reflected
now there's
another rub

COFFEEHOUSE DESPAIRS

it's only
coffeehouse despairs
that brew good poetry
at any rate
in my case
or best as I can do
which
with half of either
gary cooper's chin
or jean arthur opposite
would I think
but only
for lacking both
suffice

Holt Abandons His Monograph

holt abandons
his monograph
and returns to poetry
only to find
it isn't where he left it
it must have
rather left him
else a phantom was

A Lonely Spacious Stall

generating image
generating substance
of what difference these
of kind or of degree
a living principle
that withers to conservatism
whither this technique
or general aesthetics
withers of a horse
that can but just remember
the full fielded gallop
the wind with mane ablend
the hair too close to be a rider
the long face longer
at hooves only erstwhile shod
a lonely spacious stall
the nostrils flapping softly

SOME OTHER SUM

it's not
a numbers game
or a letters game
a zero or
some other sum
a tragic fall
triumphant rise
an equal librium
an ex's ex libris
an oh's unbelonging
and besides these
a simple grid
stalemate infinitum

THE SINGLESTANZAED POEM

you can
already see
the brushwork
so early
in the
singlestanzaed
poem
that's become
my trademark
the curves
that only
graceful strike
when seen
somewhat aslant

THAT COCKTAIL PARTY

you aim at numbers these days
the quality will take care of itself
or rather you've already done your best
there were some who glimpsed facets
openhanded the difference in indifference
but in this break in the break
I see it always was except perhaps
to meet halfway a failure
the extended hand untaken held
that cocktail party I hosted
in that physics professor's house I rented
waiting all night for the first doorbell
sinking steady and inexorable
as I've ever been since to this

BEHIND THAT CURL OF LIP

there's enjoying
what you've earned
and then there's
giving up
the question
which am or should
equivalents in action
though behind
that curl of lip
one guesses
something to distinguish
if not this work

THE MAN WHO HOLDS FORTH

the man who holds forth
holds nothing
but the fifth he bought
because he liked the word
and that kind of booze's
country of origin
virtues by association
substance and amount
in combination
all that remains of style
to any never had it

METRICALLY PERFECT

it wasn't meant
to be metrically
perfect
this life
this heart
this poem

How Simple at Heart a Creature

they finally
corrected the title
after how many
silences' discourtesy
was it that
or my wife's attention
brief but how sufficing
I told her
I told you
how simple at heart
a creature

A Little More Than Little

and what
do I leave
this as of
not my little love
grown a little
more than little
not ambition
that's
if ever was
gone
not consciousness
not history
not anything prospective
not anything else
not anything this

THE ONE BOOK I TELL

the one book
I tell everyone about
is the one
I fail to write

I Look with No Less Wonder

I look with no less wonder
at this stripmall parking lot
from this early morning café chair
attached to this antigonish hotel
than I do at the trees beyond
or the gray cotton sky beyond that
or the abstractions and suggestions
the laughing intimations as one
approaches an already perfect v
and realizing that it is perfect
and he's the wrong species besides
wheels off to a solitary treetop
where the kew kew just doesn't fit
the talons or the face

A Butterfly's Press

is it time then
to make
of one kind or another
a clean break
of bone
or of a kind of slate
with the sweep
of an arm
that would shatter or efface
with barely more
than a butterfly's press
the weight
of some thought formed
if not too perfectly
to snap

ONE WAY FAIR UNCUT

is it in
or from the rough
advantage
one way fair uncut
disadvantage other
what would
if sharper slice
this leveraged trajectory

Vita Nova Scotia

a of b
x for y
these formulae
for titles
that surpass
my most inspired
but perhaps any
vita nova scotia
would fall
all too mortal
all too human
all too any
all too else

Professor Non Grata

just how gentle
should such
an egression be
when arguments
in strength
for any answer exist
one I'd hope
not commensurate
but complementary is
to at the last lines
professor non grata

BOOKMARKS LIKE THIS

when bookmarks
like this one
are too long
they get ragged
at the top
which here suggests
given the photograph
of sunsplit clouds
representing something
beyond if not ideal
that efforts
even to glimpse
much less grasp
as mine especially any
must
as toward her aspect
prudent fall short

THIS DIMINISHED PENSCAPE

at the end
as at the beginning
the only point
is to take
another step
whether easy or hard
the taking
that's almost glib enough
to catch on
while every mouth but mine
converses
makes a sought connection
the lone exception
un seeking sought or found
looking
at a friend's unread book
beyond the scraping on
of this diminished penscape

I'M SENSING A THEME

ah that glimmer again
in this
I'm sensing a theme
café
while sits at home
in my inbox
the latest rejection
I feel a kind of resonance
potential for potential
but knowing more
and better
of being too long
in the truth
to really want for anything
hard or even flickering
fluttering anon

Should I Opt or Hope

a grace note
of foreboding
not this
but what
prompts it
for which
of the many
kinds of death
should I opt
or hope

Submitting to the Float

is it to be
away from
among the mostly
younger
so it seems
because despite
their studies
and their pensions
faces beaming
neighborly
free as unfeeling
submitting
to the float
of pleasant currents
either side

My Father's Love of Bossa Nova

you understand
the promise
and vicissitudes
of rhythm
poetry and music
music and dance
why not
dance and poetry
my father's love
of bossa nova
not reduced
but anchored
to his heart's own
arrhythmia

Tissuepaper Verse

he appears apparently
he tries tryingly
and all those
adverbial forms
that on
their verbal roots
equivocate
leaves on branches
trembling
branches' sway
on trunks
verse from resolution
like tissuepaper

WHEN IF NOT AFLOOD

I'm too
at pushing fifty
old
even
for nostalgia
the emotions
still come
sure
when
if not aflood
the right
music plays
but in
how predictable
a simpering key

FOLDFOLDFOLD

so much
of so much
is so structed
that
any other
thissed that
yearning for balance
would tear
this poem's page
and foldfoldfold it
flat
to wedge
this tableleg

In Order

george first
then paul
hardly unique
but then again
not clichéd either
is it because
you too
used to play guitar
but rocked
when you did
more tenderly than mean
or do you just
for that thus
yearn precluded ease

MY DEFINITION OF DANCE

dance is expressive
rhythmically structured
full body movement
from which you can tell
I'm in no rush to go
or anywhere home

My Own Shards and Splinters

oh
am I breaking your heart
again
it's hard not to
stepping around
my own shards and splinters
which you
for some reason
don't even notice
much less bother
to sweep up

ELSE YOU TOO SMUGLY PROCLAIM

wanting
or so disposed
I can't remember
outstretching
this body
in the void
that renders it
immobile
as if this poem
could redeem
its poet
forsake it then
else you too smugly
proclaim
this toil
as some heroic deed
this sentence
as a text

Pages of a Life Unread

if all your thoughts
come to meh
crest at meh
yield with meh
after energetic leaps
and convoluted spirals
in a pas de deux
with feeling
when all that's wanted
simpler duller
more familiar is
would you
to such syntax
feign to resort
feign to last through
the thumbflipped pages
of a life unread

When the World Wants You All In

I'd like
to entertain
the guests
the thought
the selfexpenditure
in which
masculine virtue
would consist
if I bought wholesale
or retail
some even existential
creed
that's why
limit poker
is boring but best
when the world
wants you all in

Not Even on Paper

em sym parasym
or just pathetic
fallacy
you call me
on these earnest pleas
you praise me
my shenanigans
but that's okay
it's of a piece
with the wholecloth
world
whose texture
doesn't even exist
even on paper

Which the Sadder

is it sadder
to show up
only in
the odd footnote
or
despite the dearth
when cognizant
to feel
a little thrill

WHATEVER NOW PASSES

is it
that I'm wasting
my talent
and don't care
or that
I have none
to waste
yet remain
for not trying
whatever
in this new dawn
passes for damned

WHAT THE MATTER WAS

when I asked
what the matter was
the face in the mirror
that wasn't me said
I just want
to be worthy of something
I'll never have
before closing its mouth
till now

Nonversation

so is this a con
or nonversation
and does it
on what you do
with this attempt
depend
metrical and latinate
though it's no
obligation of yours
even to at or with it
snort or wipe

This Hypermasculine Song

I notice
in this hypermasculine
song
that all the rhymes
are feminine
but that gives way
to this song
whose rhymes
as mine preferred
end with syllables
emphatic stressed
each completed couplet
feeling
to my life sentence
like the period

Slumped Abed or Asteps

is it time to
in italics
not be looked at
in that way
not your first bullfight
much as you lack
the training
familiar though
with the almost dearth
grown comfortable
with projects
the lonely consolations
last night the cat knew it
as over half a life ago
the palomino lab
slumped abed or asteps
needing and receipt

AN UNREAD CLOWN'S RICH EXCUSE

you know
that only you
are the very joke
you're laughing at
in writing this
on paper
in writing this
to publish
an unreading wife's
unread clown's
rich excuse
for legacy

GRUNT AND GLIDE TRIPPINGLY

if life is a game
then it must
after all be lost
though one
as of necessity
would seem
to go the distance
however far along
that roadunworthy
path
stone by stone
grunt and glide
trippingly along

SOMETHING LIKE RESPECT

could I beg
another pleasure
or critical review
out of
for the concepts
the ob or sub
or re the jects
something like
dislike
something like
respect

EVEN A HAIKU CAN REST

now that I've almost
I presume
learned how to live
what matters
the continuance

even a haiku
can rest as poem enough
if it be well turned

WITH APOLOGIES TO CE

do you
have
another poem
in you
well do you
punk

Hooffalls

the first time
I thought I heard a hooffall
from the park woods
was the sunpeeking overcast drizzle
the day of my father's surgery
I had he said still postop slurry
an out of body experience
they took two pounds of intestines
out of my body

the second time
I knew I'd heard a hooffall
was the next day
along not the park road
but the wooded path roadward home
the late afternoon sun
still at me with its intensity
and I stopped and stilled
and strained my squint at nothing

the third time
there was no sound
of hooffall or of else
but at the crest of that same road
from the vale vignette of regal doe
motionless in staring at me
as I then became
which juvenated to me
the frisky doe of the dykes
and before her the fawnish one
between the house and highway

OTHER ANAPHORA LITERARY PRESS TITLES

*The History of British and
American Author-Publishers*
By: Anna Faktorovich

Notes for Further Research
By: Molly Kirschner

*The Encyclopedic Philosophy of
Michel Serres*
By: Keith Moser

The Visit
By: Michael G. Casey

How to Be Happy
By: C. J. Jos

A Dying Breed
By: Scott Duff

Love in the Cretaceous
By: Howard W. Robertson

The Second of Seven
By: Jeremie Guy

CPSIA information can be obtained
at www.ICGtesting.com
Printed in the USA
LVHW110718160919
631184LV00010B/119/P